Gay Pride
Adult Coloring Book

By Beth Ingrias

Want to color more for FREE?

Get a FREE 25 page adult coloring book
visit
www.BethIngrias.com

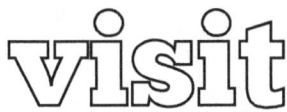

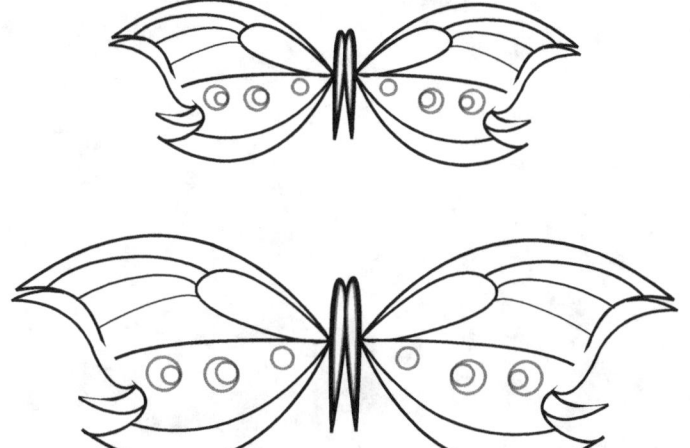

ISBN-13: 978-1-945803-51-2
ISBN-10: 1-945803-51-7

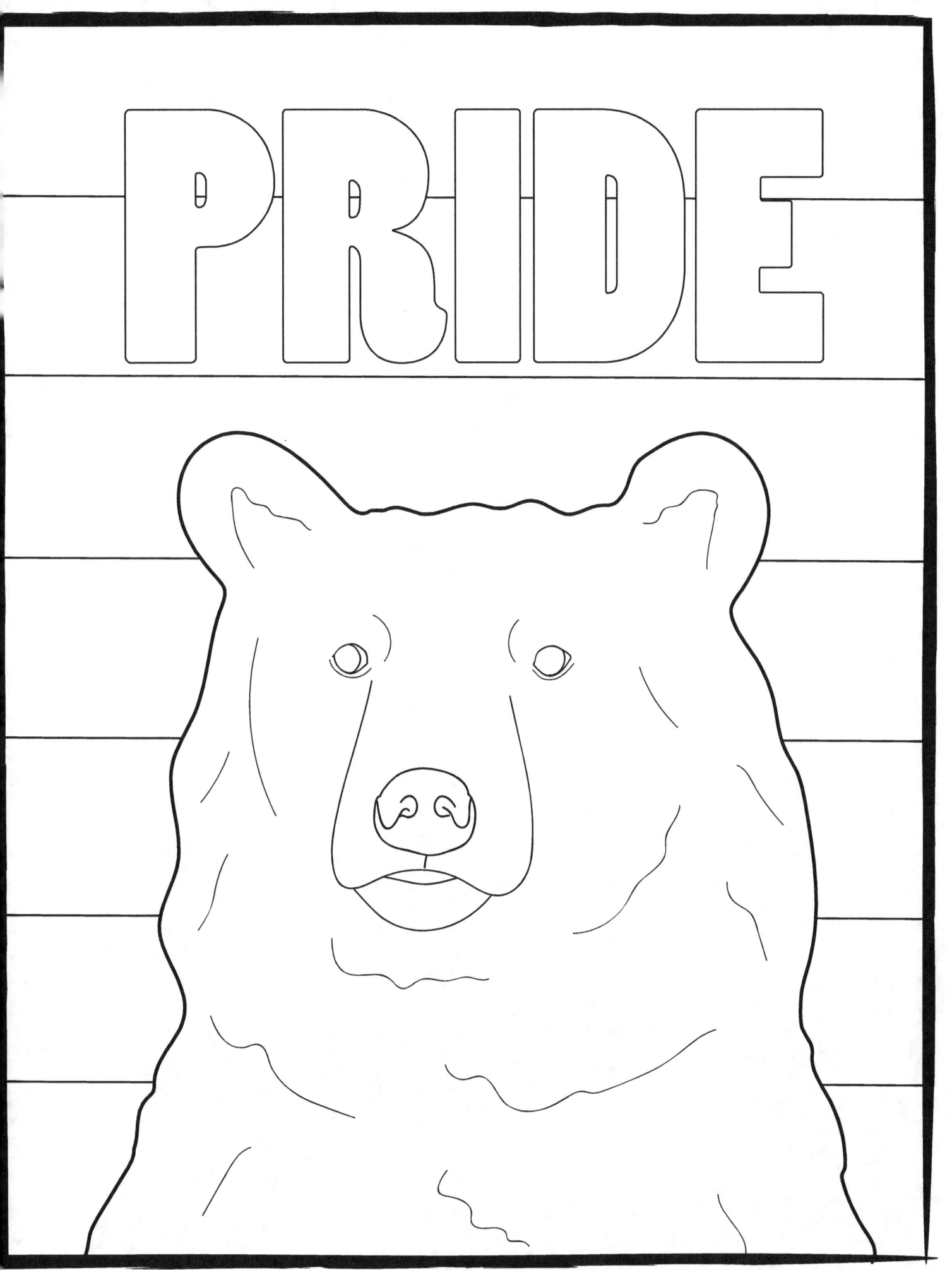

The heart wants what the heart wants

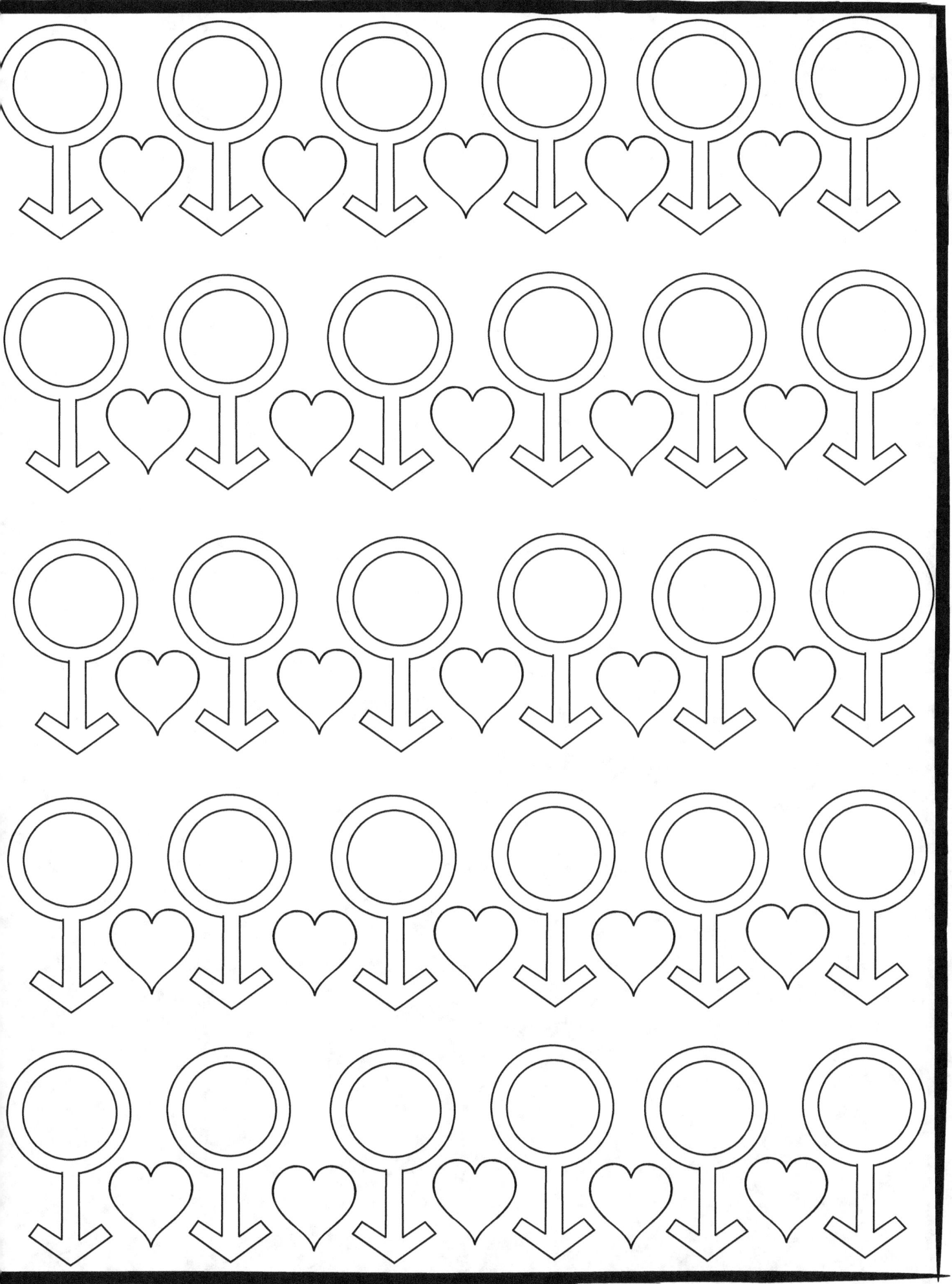

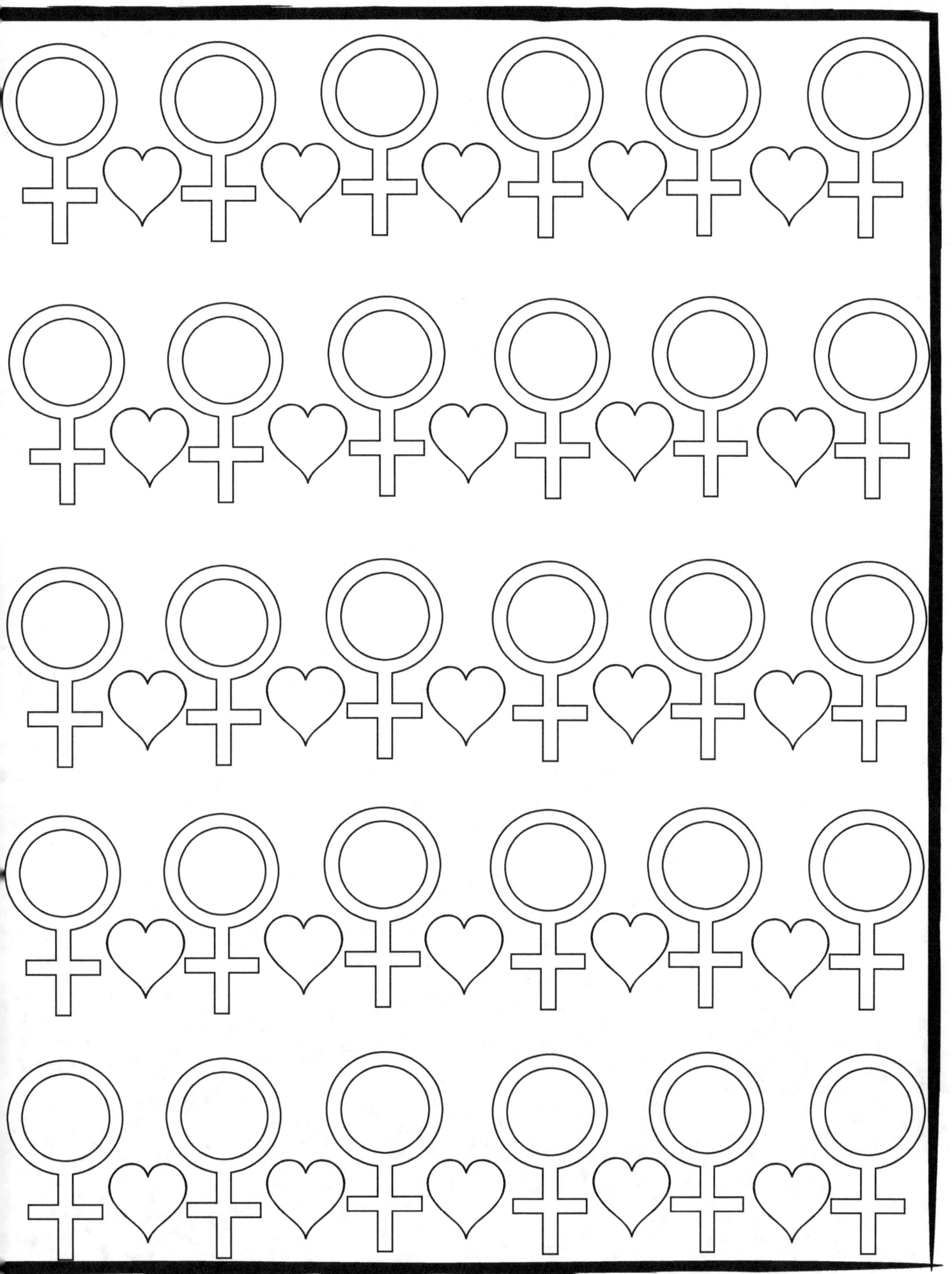

Bear

Pride

I'm so gay
I can't even
think straight

Let your love show

Love is Love

Let LOVE Win

No Shame in my Game

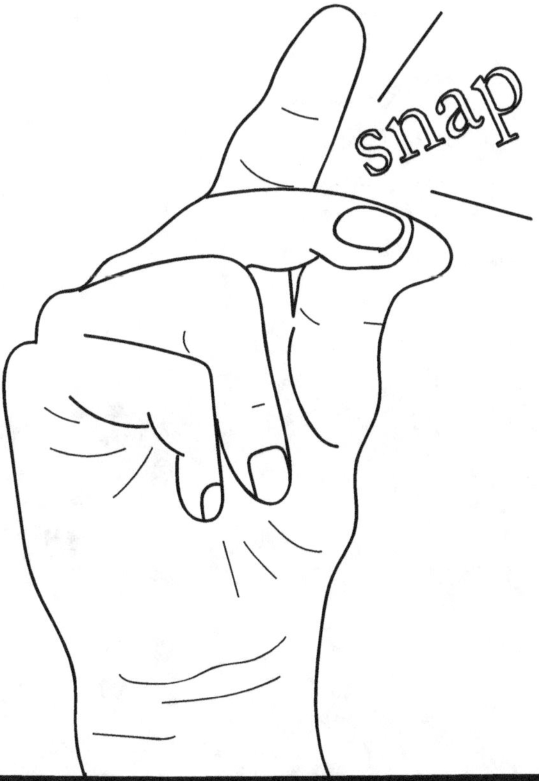

Too cute to be straight

Lipstick
Lesbian

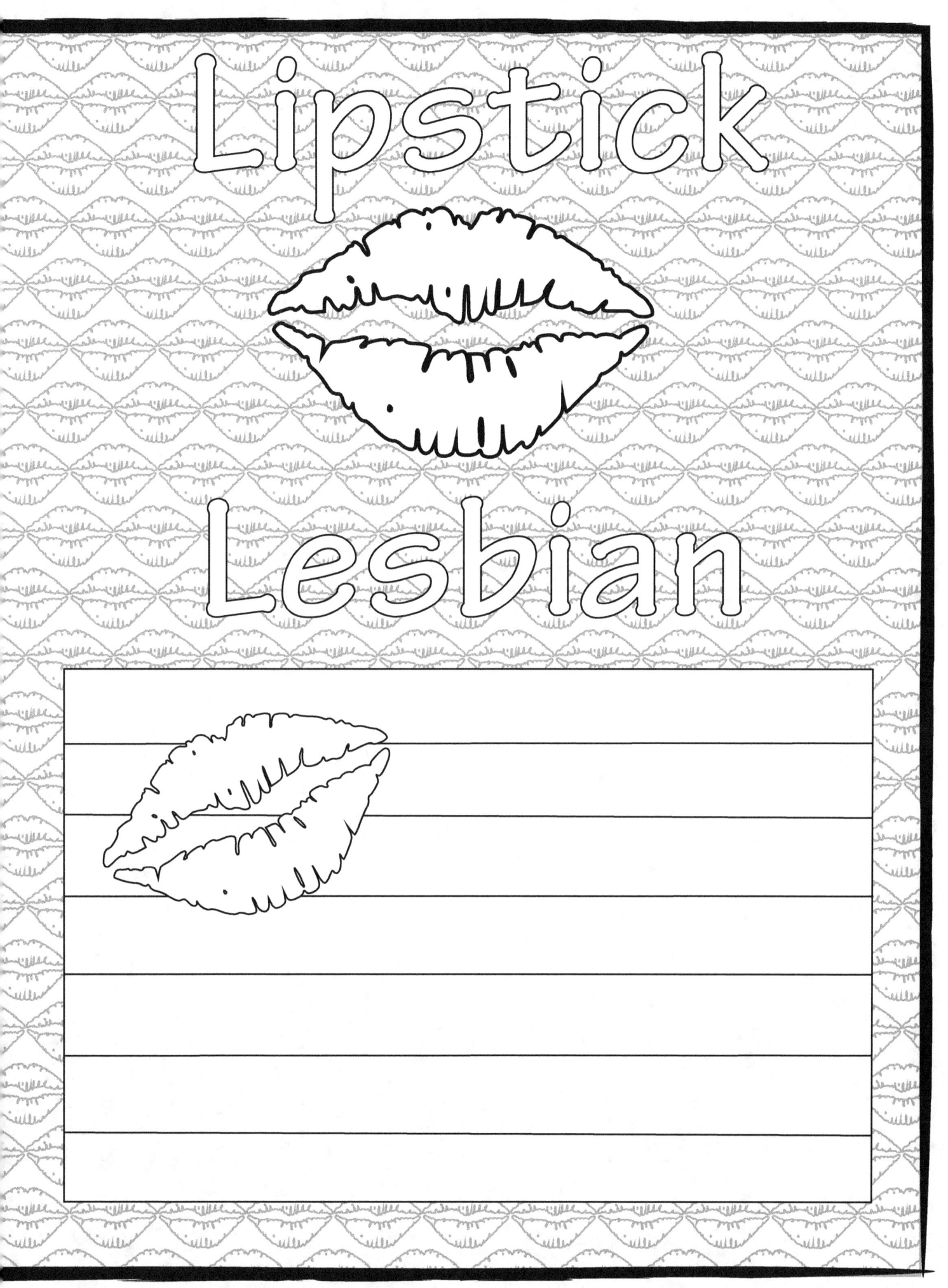

Take PRIDE in who you are and in who you LOVE

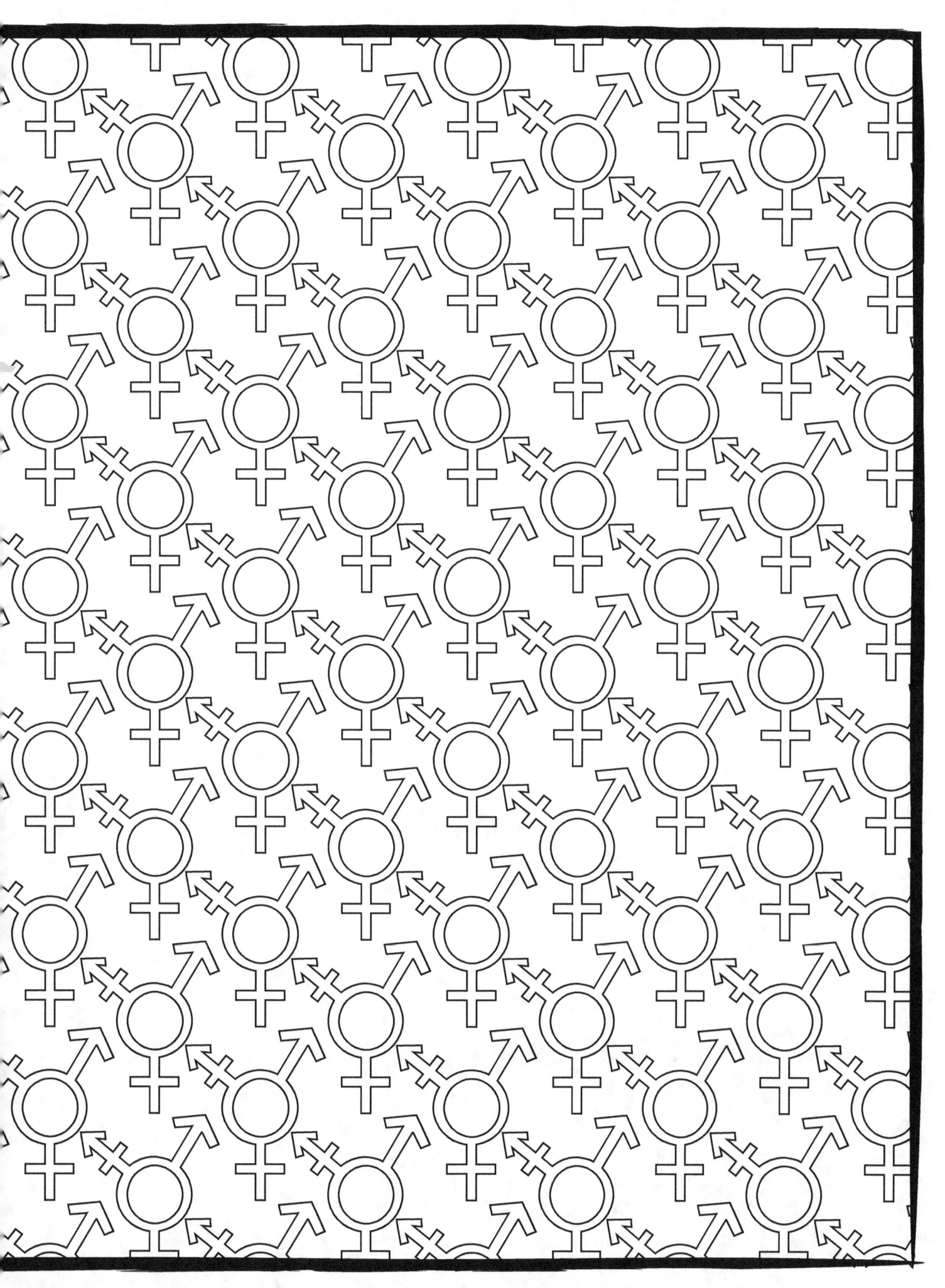

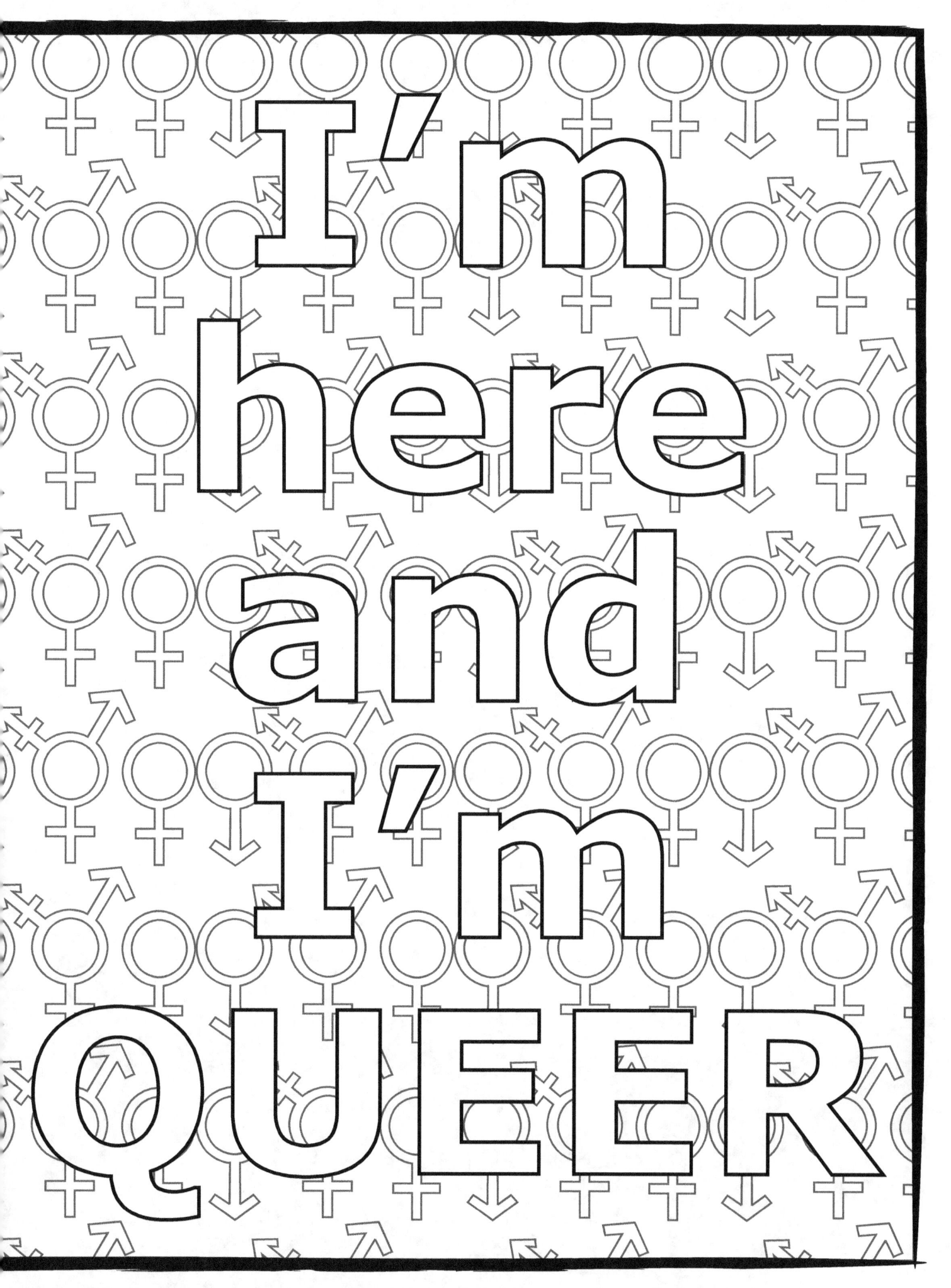

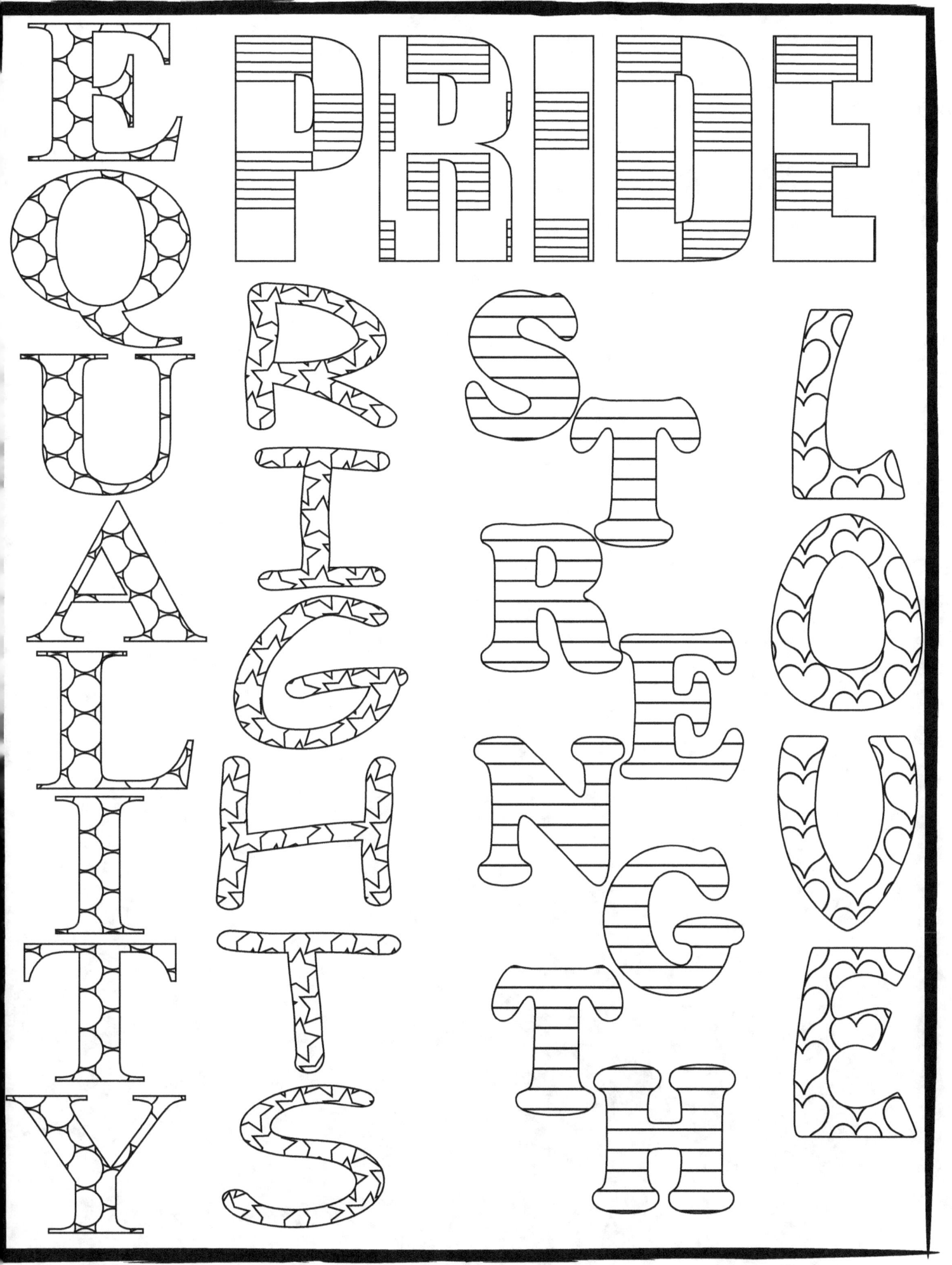

Be a Froot Loop in a world of Cheerios

Out of the closet and over the

Rainbow

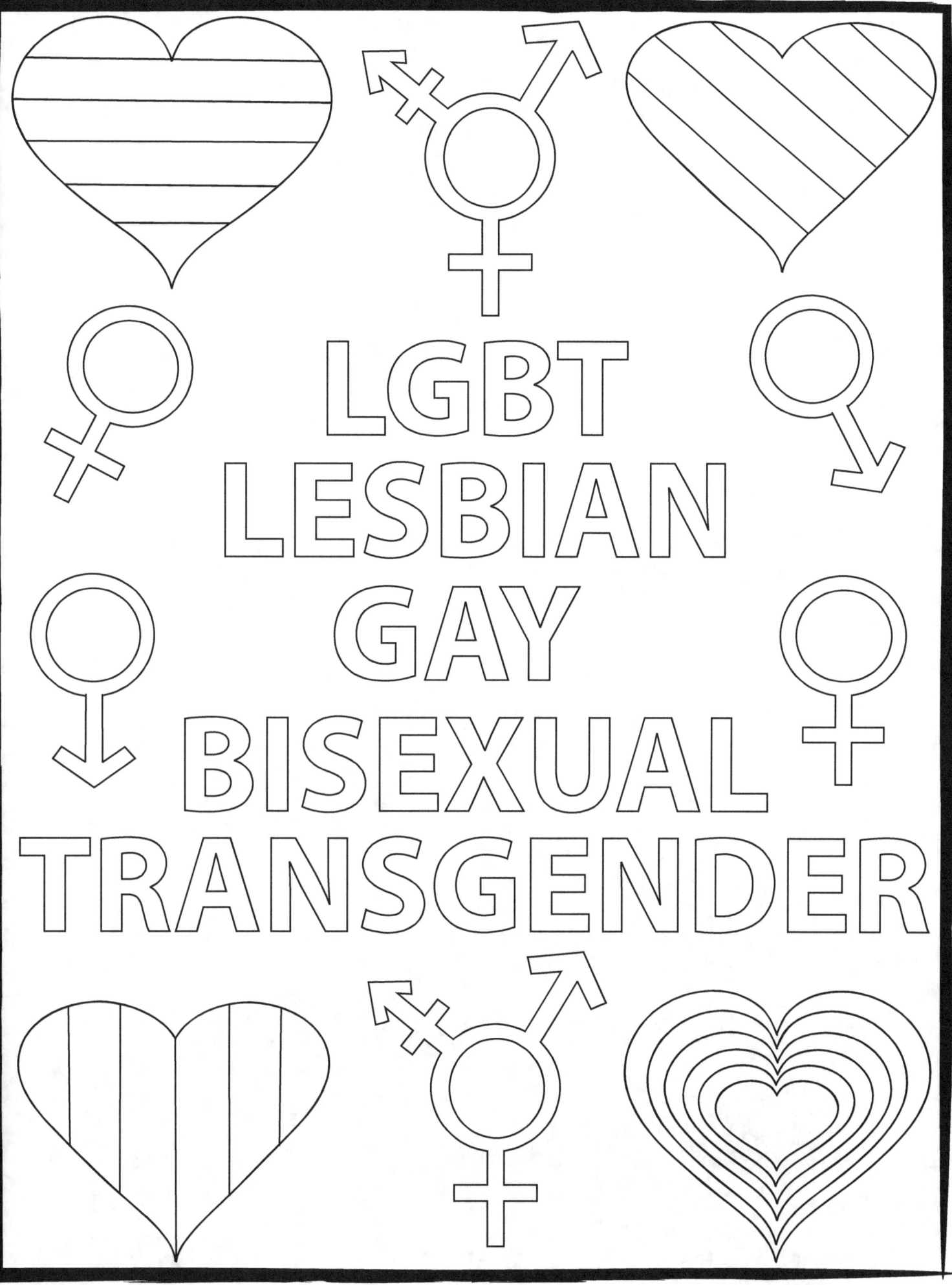